# A CourseGuide for

# Know the Heretics

## Justin Holcomb

**Z** ZONDERVAN
ACADEMIC

ZONDERVAN ACADEMIC

*A CourseGuide for Know the Heretics*
Copyright © 2020 by Zondervan

Requests for information should be addressed to:
Zondervan, *3900 Sparks Dr. SE, Grand Rapids, Michigan 49546*

ISBN 978-0-310-11096-5 (softcover)

# CONTENTS

# Introduction

Welcome to *A CourseGuide for Know the Heretics*. These guides were created for formal and informal students alike who want to engage deeper in biblical, theological, or ministry studies. We hope this guide will provide an opportunity for you to grow not only in your understanding, but also in your faith.

## How to Use This Guide

This guide is meant to be used in conjunction with the book *Know the Heretics* and its corresponding videos, *Know the Heretics Video Lectures*. After you have read each chapter in the book and watched the accompanying video lesson, the materials in this guide will help you review and assess what you have learned. Application-oriented questions are included as well.

Each CourseGuide has been individually designed to best equip you in your studies, but in general, you can expect the following components. Most CourseGuides begin every chapter with a "You Should Know" section, which highlights key terminology, people, and facts to remember. This section serves as a helpful summary for directing your studies. Reflection questions, typically two to three per chapter, prompt you to summarize key points you've learned. Discussion questions invite you to an even deeper level of engagement. Finally, most chapters will end with a short quiz to test your retention. You can find the answer key to each quiz at the bottom of the page following it.

## For Further Study

CourseGuides accompany books and videos from some of the world's top biblical and theological scholars. They may be used independently, or in small groups or classrooms, offering quality instruction to equip students for academic and ministry pursuits. If you would like to engage in further study with Zondervan's CourseGuides, the full lineup may be viewed online. After completing your studies with *A CourseGuide for Know the Heretics*, we recommend moving on to *A CourseGuide for Know How We Got Our Bible* and *A CourseGuide for Know the Creeds and Councils*.

# Introduction
*Why Heresy?*

## You Should Know

- Heretic: someone who has compromised an essential doctrine and lost sight of who God really is

- "It should be made clear that most of those dubbed heretics were usually asking legitimate and important questions."

- Clement of Alexandria wrote that heresies are a result of self-deceit and a mishandling of the Scriptures.

- Two characteristics of early heresies that tried to offer theories about God and humanity: 1) they owed too much to the spirit of the times; 2) they cut out essential parts of the Bible in order to make an explanation fit

- Five ways orthodox teaching is superior to heretical teaching: 1) it best follows the Bible; 2) it best summarizes what the Bible teaches; 3) it best accounts for paradoxes and apparent contradictions; 4) it best preserves the mystery of God in the places where reason can't go; 5) it best communicates the story of the forgiveness of the gospel

- Three fixed, nonnegotiable elements of faith that early Christians held to: 1) religious facts such as God the creator and the divine historical redeemer Christ; 2) the centrality of biblical revelation; 3) the creed and the rule of faith

## Essay Questions
### Short

1. What were some of the causes of heresy in the early church? Do you think these same factors can lead to heresy today? Why or why not?

2. What role did the rule of faith and the creeds play in responding to heresy? Are these still relevant for the church today?

3. What reasons does Holcomb give for why it is important for Christians today to study heresy? Do you find his reasons persuasive? Why or why not?

### Long

1. In your opinion, how should Christians respond to heresy today? What lessons can we learn from how the early church dealt with heresy?

## Quiz

1. The literal meaning of "orthodoxy" is _____.
   - a) Left leaning
   - b) Well meaning
   - c) Right teaching
   - d) False teaching

2. (T/F) Orthodoxy and heresy are typically determined by how many bishops or intellectuals embrace a given theory.

3. (T/F) In the early church the term "heresy" was often used to describe theological inaccuracies or imprecision.

4. The "rule of faith" was _____.
   - a) A brief summary of essential Christian truths
   - b) A guide for early Christian worship services
   - c) Another name for the Golden Rule
   - d) A reference to God's rule over Israel

5. Early Christian creeds that defined faith and refuted heresies include:
   - a) The Apostles' Creed
   - b) The Nicene Creed
   - c) The Athanasian Creed
   - d) All of the above

6. (T/F) Both the Roman Catholic and Reformed traditions have historically held that all theological errors are equally serious.

7. _____ argued that there was really no such thing as objective heresy in the early church.

    a) Bruce Demarest
    b) Walter Bauer
    c) H. E. W. Turner
    d) John Stott

8. (T/F) Heresy was responsible for the development of the doctrines of the Trinity and the nature of Christ.

9. What did C. S. Lewis call the arrogant assumption that the values and beliefs of our own time are superior to those that came before us?

    a) Heresy
    b) Orthodoxy
    c) Exceptional nonsense
    d) Chronological snobbery

10. (T/F) The early church took pains to establish a connection between its teachings and the teachings of Jesus.

# CHAPTER 1

# Judaizers

## *The Old Rules Still Apply*

### You Should Know

- Judaizers are the Jewish believers who wanted Gentiles to be circumcised and follow Jewish customs.

- Three major incidents with the Judaizers in the New Testament: 1) the circumcised believers criticizing Peter for eating with Gentiles in Acts 11; 2) the first church council in Acts 15; 3) Paul's opposition of Peter recorded in Galatians 2

- The events of Acts 15:1–2, describing the second appearance of the circumcision party: the circumcision party came to Antioch from Judea; the circumcision party taught the believers that they had to be circumcised to be saved; Paul and Barnabas had a sharp debate with the circumcision party; Paul and Barnabas were appointed to go to Jerusalem to bring the matter before the apostles and elders

- *Sozo*: the Greek word for "salvation" throughout the New Testament

- By giving the Holy Spirit to non-Jews without first converting them to Jewish practices God indicated to the church that he had discarded the old categories of Jew and non-Jew.

- The ways Jesus is a better version of the elements the Judaizers found appealing in Old Judaism: 1) Christ is the Chosen One; 2) Christ is the true circumcision; 3) Christ is the true Sabbath 4) Christ is the true guilt-offering

- "I do not set aside the grace of God, for if righteousness could be gained through the law, Christ died for nothing!" (Galatians 2:21).

## Essay Questions

### Short

1. Why did Peter and Paul believe God had accepted the Gentiles? What response did Peter and Paul receive when they shared this? How do you think the Judaizers might have responded to them?

2. In what ways does Christ fulfill the Old Testament law?

3. What is Paul's twofold response to the Judaizers? Which passage listed in each of the two categories do you resonate with most? Why?

### Long

1. Summarize the three incidents with the Judaizers in the New Testament. Do you see any parallels between these incidents and issues the church is dealing with today?

## Quiz

1. (T/F) Jesus's life and ministry shows that he was concerned about the Jewish people of Israel but not about Gentiles.

2. There are _____ major incidents with the Judaizers in the New Testament.
   a) 3
   b) 5
   c) 7
   d) 9

3. The Judaizers were also known as the _____.
   a) Outlaws
   b) Baptizers
   c) Circumcision Party
   d) Zealots

4. (T/F) Paul once criticized Peter for refusing to eat with uncircumcised believers.

5. What teaching of the Judaizers led to the first church council described in Acts 15?

a) Baptism is necessary for salvation
b) Temple worship is necessary for salvation
c) Keeping the sabbath is necessary for salvation
d) Circumcision is necessary for salvation

6. (T/F) Peter coined the term "Judaizer" in the Gospel of John.

7. (T/F) The Judaizers drew most of their beliefs from pagan philosophy.

8. Paul told the Galatians who were trying to be justified by the law that they had _____.

a) Fallen away from grace
b) Set the bar high
c) Done the best they could
d) Celebrated too soon

9. _____ is a central reason Martin Luther took issue with the Roman Catholic Church of his day.

a) Salvation by works alone
b) The doctrine of purgatory
c) Biblical inerrancy
d) Grace by faith alone

10. (T/F) It is not by works that we are saved, but solely by the grace of Christ.

ANSWER KEY
1. F, 2. A, 3. C, 4. T, 5. D, 6. F, 7. F, 8. A, 9. D, 10. T

# CHAPTER 2

# Gnostics

## *God Hides Messages for the Enlightened*

### You Should Know

- Besides a belief in hidden knowledge, other characteristics that bound different Gnostic groups: 1) the belief that matter is evil; 2) the belief that spirit is pure; 3) the belief in an elaborate primordial mythology

- *Against Heresies*, written by Irenaeus, described and refuted Gnostic beliefs.

- The elements of the "pyramid" of the Gnostic myth: the supreme transcendent god who lives in "silent silence"; a divine mother; Aeons (lesser gods); numerous less good and less powerful gods; Archons (evil gods)

- The content of the Gnostic gospel was an attempt to rouse the soul from its sleep-walking condition and to make it aware of the high destiny to which it is called.

- *Gnosis*: the Greek word for "knowledge"

- Christology: the teaching about the person and work of Christ

### Essay Questions

#### Short

1. Explain what Gnostics believed about their supreme being (theology), and their beliefs about human beings (anthropology). How do these beliefs contrast with the teachings of Scripture?

2. What did Gnostics believe about who Jesus was? What did Gnostics believe about Jesus's death and what it accomplished? How do they contrast with the biblical view?

3. How did Irenaeus respond to the Gnostics? What do you find most interesting about his response?

### Long

1. Summarize the key beliefs of the Gnostics. How did Paul and the early Christians respond to the Gnostics? Why do you think Gnostic beliefs appealed to people?

## Quiz

1. (T/F) Gnosticism is not a specific heretical movement in church history but rather a loose collection of different religious beliefs.

2. (T/F) The letters of Paul as well as 1 John contain anti-Gnostic warnings.

3. A collection of Gnostic texts was discovered a few decades ago near _____ in Egypt.

    a) The pyramids
    b) The Sphinx
    c) Nag Hammadi
    d) Cairo

4. (T/F) The Gnostics believed that faith in Christ was the way to salvation.

5. Gnostics believed in numerous dark, evil gods known as _____, and the God of the Hebrew Bible was one of these gods.

    a) Archons
    b) Leptons
    c) Aeons
    d) Positrons

6. Because Gnosticism borrowed from other religions, its _____ character makes it hard to define.

    a) Parasitic

    b) Deceptive

    c) Creative

    d) Heretical

7. The Gnostic evil, creator god Yaldabaoth was meant to be identified with _____.

    a) The Roman god Zeus

    b) The Greek god Ares

    c) The Egyptian god Horus

    d) The God of Israel

8. (T/F) Gnostics taught that Jesus was a great teacher who was fully human, rather than divine.

9. Gnostics dismissed _____ because of its/their stories of anger, war, and vengeance.

    a) The *Iliad*

    b) The four gospels

    c) The Hebrew Bible

    d) The letters of Paul

10. The popular book _____ is an example of the recent renaissance of Gnostic spirituality.

    a) *Harry Potter and the Philosopher's Stone*

    b) *The Secret*

    c) *The Hunger Games*

    d) *The Girl on the Train*

# CHAPTER 3

# Marcion

## *Vengeful Yahweh versus Gentle Jesus*

### You Should Know

- The early Christian writers who condemned Marcion: Polycarp, Justin, Irenaeus, Clement, Tertullian, Hippolytus, Pseudo-Tertullian, Bardesanes, and Origen

- Marcion believed that the God who gave the law could not be the God who gave the gospel.

- Richard Dawkins stated that "the God of the Old Testament is arguably the most unpleasant character in all fiction."

- Marcion: the son of a Christian bishop and a teacher in Rome

- Dualism: a worldview that pits two basic realities against each other

- Tertullian: a leader of the church in North Africa

### Essay Questions

#### Short

1. What contradictions did Marcion see between passages in the Old Testament and the New Testament? How was Marcion's Bible different from the traditional Christian Bible?

2. How did Tertullian and Irenaeus respond to Marcion?

3. What doctrines did the church clarify as a result of Marcion's teaching? Why were these clarifications important?

*Long*

1. Summarize Marcion's heretical teachings. How do these contrast with the teachings of Scripture? Why are Marcion's teachings still relevant to the church today?

## Quiz

1. (T/F) As a result of Marcion's views, he was excommunicated from the church.

2. (T/F) According to Marcion, the God of the Old Testament is a benevolent deity who sent Jesus to save the world.

3. (T/F) Marcion's influence stretched around the Mediterranean and lasted for two hundred years.

4. (T/F) Marcion thought that Yahweh of the Old Testament and Jesus of the New Testament were bitter enemies.

5. Marcion rejected all _____ interpretations of Scripture.
    a) Logical
    b) Allegorical
    c) Local
    d) Spiritual

6. Tertullian questioned Marcion's authority because he had no _____.
    a) Official papers from the church
    b) Followers who accepted his message
    c) Training from a recognized bishop
    d) Connection to the earliest Christians

7. Tertullian criticized Marcion's followers for their addiction to _____, since it contradicted their opposition to creation.
    a) Food
    b) Wine
    c) Science
    d) Astrology

8. Irenaeus criticized Marcion for removing the narratives about Jesus's birth from _____.

    a) The gospel of Luke
    b) The gospel of Matthew
    c) The book of Acts
    d) The book of Romans

9. Tertullian argued in *Against Marcion* that the two Testaments of the Bible are _____.

    a) Contradictory
    b) Written by different divine beings
    c) Not contradictory
    d) Two sides of the same coin

10. (T/F) According to historian Philip Schaff, Marcion's view implies that God was actively involved in creation from the beginning until the time of Christ.

# CHAPTER 4

# Docetists

## The Spiritual Is Good, the Physical Is Evil

### You Should Know

- Why did philosophers of the early centuries of Christianity struggle to accept Jesus's humanity? They thought pure spirit couldn't mix with corrupt flesh.

- According to New Testament scholar Rudolf Bultmann, "The resurrection itself is not an event of past history."

- Ebionitism: a movement that regarded Jesus as an ordinary human being

- Docetism: the belief that Jesus was totally divine and that his humanity was merely an appearance

- Incarnation: the union of divinity and humanity in Jesus

### Essay Questions

#### Short

1. How did the Docetists describe Jesus's life and "death"? How do these teachings contrast with Scripture?

2. How did Irenaeus respond to the Docetic denial of the Incarnation? What are your thoughts about his response?

3. What Scriptural evidence is there that Jesus was a true human being? Why do you think many Christians struggle with accepting Jesus's full humanity?

*Long*

1. Describe Docetic beliefs. How do these beliefs contrast with Scripture? In your view, what is the greatest danger that Docetism presents? In what ways does Docetic thinking manifest itself today?

## Quiz

1. (T/F) Docetism derives from the Greek verb "to question."

2. (T/F) Docetism originated with Docetus, a teacher who lived in Rome.

3. The apocryphal _____ illustrates a Docetic view of Christ's sufferings.

    a) Gospel of Thomas
    b) Gospel of John
    c) Book of Judith
    d) Gospel of Peter

4. (T/F) Docetism developed to make Christianity more acceptable to pagan societies.

5. (T/F) In the gospel of Matthew, Jesus states, "I did not die in reality but in appearance."

6. _____ was one of the first leaders to defend orthodoxy against Docetism. (p. 57)

    a) Richard Dawkins
    b) Ignatius of Antioch
    c) Simon of Cyrene
    d) Marcion

7. One document influenced by Docetism states that _____ was crucified instead of Jesus.

    a) Judas
    b) John
    c) Ignatius of Antioch
    d) Simon of Cyrene

8. (T/F) Salvation depends on Christ's really being a man who suffered and was resurrected.

9. Irenaeus was especially critical of the prominent Docetic teacher _____.

    a) Valentinus
    b) Docetus
    c) Polycarp
    d) Stephen

10. _____ typically holds that supernatural elements in the Bible are not historical but mythical.

    a) Orthodoxy
    b) Liberalism
    c) Docetism
    d) Marcionism

# CHAPTER 5

# Mani

## *God Must Be Freed*

## You Should Know

- The religions that Mani borrowed from to create his belief system: Christianity; Buddhism; Zoroastrianism

- The beliefs of the Elchaisites, the Jewish-Christian sect that Mani grew up in: a strict interpretation of the Jewish law; a belief in Christ as a divine teacher; a kosher diet; deep reverence for the environment; baptism

- Reasons that Manichaeans were persecuted by various governments: they were pacifists; they lived introspectively; they practiced a number of alien rituals

- The Manichaean Elect were promised immediate access to the afterlife and being made into angels if they remained faithful.

- For Mani, the key to salvation was separation: The divine spirit was confined in the material world and needed to be released.

- Zoroastrian dualism: the idea that good and evil are locked in an eternal battle, with neither side having the upper hand

## Essay Questions

### *Short*

1. Describe the cosmology of the Manichaeans. How does it differ from the cosmology of the Bible?

2. Why do you think Manichaeanism appealed to some people more than orthodox Christianity?

3. How did Augustine defend the Old Testament against Manichaean attacks? Do you find his response persuasive? Why or why not?

### Long

1. Summarize the orthodox response to the Manichaeans. Which points of response do you find most compelling? Do these responses raise any additional questions for you? What can Christians today learn from Manichaean beliefs and practices?

## Quiz

1. (T/F) Mani believed that matter was inherently good while the spiritual realm was evil.

2. Mani claimed to have a vision in which an angel told him that God had chosen him as the _____.
   a) Messiah
   b) King
   c) Prophet
   d) Paraclete

3. (T/F) Mani believed that the Old Testament was superior to the New Testament.

4. (T/F) Manichaeans were generally welcomed in the lands in which they settled.

5. According to Mani, redemption involved awakening a _____ rather than restoring a fallen nature.
   a) Sleeping giant
   b) Sleeping cosmos
   c) Sleeping God
   d) Sleeping religion

6. (T/F) The main task of the Elect was to free the pieces of God that were trapped in plants by eating them.

7. (T/F) Manichaeans were strong proponents of the resurrection of the dead.

8. _____, a North African bishop, adhered to Manichaeanism for ten years before he converted to Christianity.

    a) St. Augustine
    b) Faustus
    c) Mani
    d) Irenaeus

9. (T/F) Manichaeans were known for defending their belief in Jesus's incarnation.

10. (T/F) Manichaeanism no longer directly influences any major religion today.

# CHAPTER 6

# Sabellius

## *One Actor and Three Hats*

### You Should Know

- By prioritizing oneness, Modalists were voting for continuity with Judaism and, in particular, with Jewish monotheism.

- The Sabellians maintained that any Scripture passage that suggested that God is more than one must be interpreted metaphorically.

- Three orthodox theologians who responded to the challenge of Sabellianism and hammered out the basics of Trinitarian theology: Hippolytus, Tertullian, and Origen

- Three pieces of evidence that Tertullian gave that Jesus was a distinct person from the Father: Christ did not know when the end of the world would take place, but the Father did; Christ was forsaken by the Father on the cross; Jesus constantly pointed his listeners to the Father as well as himself

- Sabellius: a third-century theologian and priest

- Modalism: a heresy that claims that the Father, Son, and Holy Spirit are different modes of God

### Essay Questions

#### *Short*

1. How did Sabellius understand the relationship between the one God and the Father, Son, and Holy Spirit?

2. How did Sabellius answer the following questions: 1) Who was crucified on the cross and 2) Who was Jesus speaking to when he referred to God as the Father?

3. Restate the excerpt from the Athanasian Creed in your own words. How does this excerpt illuminate your understanding of the Trinity?

*Long*

1. What was the Sabellian heresy and how did the early church leaders respond to it? What new insights did you gain from this section in relation to God being both one and three?

## Quiz

1. _____, a heresy, emerged as a response to the polytheistic culture that the early Christians lived in.
   a) Docetism
   b) Monarchianism
   c) Marcionism
   d) All of the above

2. (T/F) Sabellius argued that Jesus had genuine conversations with God the Father while Jesus was on earth.

3. (T/F) A number of Sabellius's writings have survived to the present day.

4. (T/F) Sabellianism lacked clout as a movement and never made much headway into the church proper.

5. _____ excommunicated Sabellius and ended Sabellius's career in the public eye. (p. 81)
   a) Tertullian
   b) Origen
   c) Augustine
   d) Pope Callistus

6. (T/F) In theology, it is much easier to tell when an idea is wrong than to articulate the right answer.

7. (T/F) The challenge of Sabellianism motivated the first substantial Trinitarian theologies and generated the terms we use today.

8. _____ proposed that we speak of the Godhead as one substance consisting in three persons.

    a) Tertullian
    b) Sabellius
    c) Mani
    d) Luther

9. Tertullian argued that when Jesus said, "I and my Father are one," he was emphasizing the idea of _____, or divine essence.

    a) Faith
    b) Love
    c) Substance
    d) Grace

10. (T/F) Mormons and Jehovah's Witnesses are known for their Trinitarian doctrine.

# CHAPTER 7

# Arius

## *Jesus Is a Lesser God*

## You Should Know

- Arius concluded that only God the Father is without beginning. The Son came into existence through the will of the Father.

- Athanasius was the foremost defender of Nicene orthodoxy and a prolific writer of orthodox Trinitarian doctrine in the fourth century.

- Basil the Great, Gregory of Nyssa, and Gregory of Nazianzus were the friends of Athanasius, the Cappadocian fathers, who continued the fight against Arianism after Athanasius died.

- Arius: a presbyter in Alexandria who taught that Jesus was separate from the Father

- Adoptionism: the idea that a human person named Jesus was adopted into divinity

- Immutability: the belief that God does not change

## Essay Questions

### *Short*

1. How did Arius's Greek philosophical presuppositions influence his understanding of Jesus? Is it important for us to be aware of our own presuppositions when we interpret Scripture?

2. What happened at the Council of Nicaea in AD 325? Did Arianism fade away after this council met?

3. What criticisms did Athanasius make against Arius? In your opinion, which is the strongest, and why?

### Long

1. Describe the Arian heresy. How did orthodox church leaders respond? Why were leaders like Athanasius determined to defend the full deity of Jesus? Are there any groups claiming to be Christian who deny Jesus's divinity today?

## Quiz

1. (T/F) Arius firmly embraced Sabellius's Modalism.

2. (T/F) Part of Arius's responsibility as a presbyter was to direct a school of biblical interpretation for priests and laypersons.

3. (T/F) A riot broke out when followers of Arius and followers of Alexander met in the streets.

4. "_____" was not a common term at the time Arius lived.
   a) Heresy
   b) Bishop
   c) Trinity
   d) Synod

5. Origen wrote that the Son is _____ to the Father.
   a) Partially related
   b) Closely related
   c) Eternally faithful
   d) Eternally subordinate

6. (T/F) Most early theologians believed that God could not suffer.

7. (T/F) Emperor Constantine called the Council of Nicaea in AD 325.

8. According to _____, the Son was eternally begotten from the Father and thus was of the same essence with the Father. (p. 93)
   a) Athanasius
   b) Constantine
   c) Arius
   d) Paul of Samosata

9. _____ thought the Semi-Arian view could be a good compromise between the Arians and the orthodox doctrines. (94)

   a) Athanasius
   b) Arius
   c) Tertullian
   d) Constantius

10. (T/F) Athanasius had to endure five exiles.

# CHAPTER 8

# Apollinarius

## *Christ May Be Human, but His Mind Is Divine*

- Three ways that Apollinarius referred to Christ: God-incarnate, flesh-bearing God, God born into a woman

- Apollinarius denied that Christ had a human will, because he believed a human will was inherently sinful.

- The frankly acknowledged presupposition of Apollinarius's argument is that the divine Word was substituted for the normal human psychology in Christ.

- Council of Chalcedon: provided a definition of the relationship of the human and divine in Christ

- Gregory of Nazianzus: a fourth-century Archbishop of Constantinople devoted to orthodox Trinitarian theology

### Essay Questions

#### Short

1. What question led to the Council of Chalcedon (AD 451) being called? What is the danger of seeing Jesus as two distinct persons? What is the danger of overemphasizing the unity of his person?

2. What was Apollinarius's heresy? Why did he believe it? What negative implications did it have for Christian theology?

3. What did Gregory of Nazianzus mean when he wrote, "What has not been assumed has not been healed"? Why did Gregory of Nazianzus argue that it was important for Christ to have a human intellect? How did he relate this issue to the doctrine of the Trinity?

### Long

1. What was the Apollinarian heresy and how did early Christian leaders respond? Why do you think this heresy was attractive to people?

## Quiz

1. (T/F) Apollinarius appealed to Nicaea and emphasized the full deity of Jesus Christ.

2. Apollinarius was influenced by _____ and understood human nature to be composed of a body, a soul, and a mind.
   a) Athanasius
   b) Alexander
   c) Plato
   d) Nicaea

3. (T/F) Apollinarius believed that the *Logos*, or eternal Son, replaced the soul that would have existed in the person of Jesus Christ.

4. (T/F) Apollinarius acknowledged that he was teaching a new doctrine, but claimed it was better than the old doctrine.

5. (T/F) Pope Damasus held a council in 377 and cleared Apollinarius of all the charges against him.

6. The Council of _____ in 381 put the nails in the coffin of Apollinarianism.
   a) Constantinople
   b) Nicaea
   c) Damasus
   d) Philadelphia

7. _____ famously wrote, "What has not been assumed has not been healed."

    a)  Athanasius
    b)  Basil the Great
    c)  Apollinarius
    d)  Gregory of Nazianzus

8. (T/F) Gregory of Nazianzus argued that it wasn't important whether or not Jesus possessed a functioning human mind.

9. (T/F) The Gospels depict Jesus as being completely human.

10. (T/F) New Testament scholar John A. T. Robinson claimed that most modern orthodox Christians hold an Apollinarian view of the personhood of Christ.

# CHAPTER 9

# Pelagius

## *God Has Already Given Us the Tools*

### You Should Know

- Two beliefs Christians in the first four centuries held concerning human nature: humanity is fallen and requires divine help for salvation; humans have a will and are responsible for their sin

- The starting point of Pelagius's moralistic theology was his insistence that God would never command anything that is impossible for humans to carry out.

- Pelagius objected to Augustine's prayer in Augustine's book *Confessions*, because he thought it turned humans into puppets determined by God's action.

- The things Augustine kept at the center of his theology toward the end of his life: the sovereignty of God, human depravity, humanity's need of grace

- Justification by faith: the idea that believing and trusting in Christ is the way to salvation

### Essay Questions

#### *Short*

1. What did Pelagius believe about human nature and the doctrine of original sin? What was Pelagius's understanding of the freedom of the will?

2. What did Augustine believe about the freedom of the will? Which approach do you find more convincing—Augustine's or Pelagius's?

3. What did Augustine believe about original sin? Is there evidence of the effects of original sin in our world today?

### Long

1. What was the Pelagian heresy? What key errors did Pelagius make in his theology? How did Augustine respond to Pelagius? Which of Augustine's criticisms do you find most compelling? How is the Pelagian controversy still relevant today?

## Quiz

1. (T/F) Pelagius was Trinitarian and held to the divinity and humanity of Christ.

2. (T/F) Pelagius urged people to reform their behavior and live as upstanding moral citizens.

3. Pelagius's teaching was condemned by the _____ in 431.
    a) Council of Ephesus
    b) Council of Chalcedon
    c) Council of Toledo
    d) Council of Alexandria

4. (T/F) Pelagius interpreted Matthew 5:48 to mean that perfection is within our reach.

5. (T/F) Pelagius was a strong defender of the doctrine of original sin.

6. When Pelagius spoke of grace, he meant _____.
    a) The way we should show tolerance to each other
    b) God's supernatural power in our lives
    c) Our natural ability to obey God
    d) God's forgiveness

7. _____ is famous for opposing Pelagianism in many of his major works.

    a) Mani
    b) Arius
    c) Augustine
    d) Leo the Great

8. (T/F) Augustine said that, after the fall, all humans were guilty of Adam's sin.

9. (T/F) Augustine held that if Adam had not sinned, he would not have died.

10. The theology of Augustine formally won against Pelagianism at the _____ in 418.

    a) Council of Chalcedon
    b) Council of Toledo
    c) Council of Alexandria
    d) Council of Carthage

# CHAPTER 10

# Eutyches
## *Christ as a New Kind of Being*

### You Should Know

- Cyril, Bishop of Alexandria, said of Christ's two natures, "A distinction of the natures is necessary, a division is reprehensible."

- The four most powerful bishops during the Eutychian controversy, who were known as the patriarchs, were the bishops of Alexandria, Antioch, Constantinople, and Rome.

- The Second Council of Ephesus reaffirmed Eutyches's theology and he was restored to his former position.

- The "four fences" the "Definition of Chalcedon" placed around the person of Christ in relation to his two natures: without confusion, without change, without division, without separation

- The bishops at Chalcedon labored hard to craft a careful statement that distinguished Christ's two natures in his one person, because salvation depends on both natures of Christ.

- *Eranistes*: a theological dialogue written by Theodoret of Cyrus that criticized Eutychianism

### Essay Questions
*Short*

1. Summarize the historical background to the Eutychian controversy. How did Eutyches understand the relationship between the two natures of Christ?

2. What happened at the Council of Chalcedon? What did it accomplish?

3. Why did the orthodox theologians fight to preserve a recognition of Jesus's human nature? What did they believe was at stake?

*Long*

1. What was Eutyches's theological error? How did orthodox church leaders respond? What is your opinion about the political drama that went on behind the scenes?

## Quiz

1. (T/F) Dioscorus succeeded Cyril as bishop of Alexandria in 444.

2. (T/F) Eutyches described Christ as one new and different person fashioned out of two natures.

3. Leo the Great's letter that condemned Eutyches's theology came to be known as _____.

    a) Eutyches's Folly
    b) The Great Takedown
    c) Leo's "Tome"
    d) A Defense of Orthodoxy

4. Leo of Rome famously dubbed the second council of Ephesus _____.

    a) "The Great Escape"
    b) "The Robber Synod"
    c) "The Worst of all Councils"
    d) "The Final Event"

5. A fourth ecumenical council met at _____ to replace the second council of Ephesus.

    a) Chalcedon
    b) Trier
    c) Rome
    d) Paris

6. (T/F) The Council of Chalcedon sought to bridge the gap between the Alexandrian and Antiochene schools.

7. (T/F) Leo the Great accused Eutyches of teaching another form of Docetism.

8. In the end, the Council of Chalcedon recognized that Jesus Christ is one person who exists with two _____.

    a) Angels at his side
    b) Spirits
    c) Distinguishable natures
    d) Minds

9. The definition crafted by the Chalcedonian council made sure to exclude Eutychianism and _____ from any place in orthodox Christianity.

    a) Nestorianism
    b) Vitalism
    c) Legalism
    d) Marcionism

10. (T/F) The orthodox theologians of the first several centuries held that there was little connection between the incarnation and the atoning work of Christ.

ANSWER KEY

1. T, 2. T, 3. C, 4. B, 5. A, 6. T, 7. T, 8. C, 9. A, 10. F

# CHAPTER 11

# Nestorius

## Christ's Divinity Must Be Shielded

### You Should Know

- For Nestorius, Jesus Christ had and maintained two natures and two persons.

- The reasons Nestorius believed it was important to distinguish two persons in Jesus: it explained why Jesus was ignorant of certain events that God would have known; it protected the impassability of God (i.e., his inability to suffer)

- What did Cyril find most troubling about Nestorius's two-nature theory about Jesus? The humanity of Jesus could be so opaque that his divinity would not shine through.

- The results of the First Council of Ephesus: the term *Theotokos* was officially approved;

- Nestorius was stripped of his power and rank and exiled; a schism developed between the church of Antioch and the church of Alexandria

- Monophysitism: the heresy that Jesus had one merged divine-human nature

- *Communicatio idiomatum*: communication of properties

### Essay Questions

#### Short

1. What question about Christ was the church debating in the time of Nestorius? What was the difference between the Alexandrian and Antiochene schools on this issue?

2. What dilemma did Nestorius try to solve by positing that Christ consisted of two persons? How did he see his model solving this problem?

3. What concerns did Cyril, Patriarch of Alexandria, have about Nestorius's views?

### Long

1. Why did Cyril and other church leaders oppose Nestorius's two-person view of Christ? Why is it important to maintain the unity of Christ's personhood? What would the implications be if Jesus were both a human and divine person, as Nestorius claimed?

### Quiz

1. (T/F) The Council of Nicaea (325) codified the position that Christ was both God and man.

2. The two main theological schools of thought in relation to Jesus's divinity and humanity were the Alexandrian school and the _____ school.

   a) Arian
   b) Antiochene
   c) Orthodox
   d) Syrian

3. (T/F) Nestorius was appointed Patriarch of Constantinople in 428.

4. Nestorius considered _____ the most fitting title for Mary, the mother of Jesus.

   a) Eternal Virgin
   b) *Theotokos*
   c) *Christotokos*
   d) *Anthropotokos*

5. Nestorius acknowledged that he developed his Christology in light of the major heresies of Arianism and _____.

   a) Pelagianism
   b) Gnosticism

c) Manichaeanism
d) Docetism

6. (T/F) The chief opponent of Nestorius was the emperor Theodosius II.

7. (T/F) Cyril believed that Nestorius's theory threatened the idea of Jesus as "God among us."

8. (T/F) Cyril's motives for criticizing Nestorius were purely doctrinal.

9. The meeting later known as _____ was the climax of the conflict between Cyril and Nestorius.

a) The First Council of Ephesus
b) The Council of Nicaea
c) The Robber Synod
d) The Council of Antioch

10. (T/F) The Council of Chalcedon (451) retracted the condemnation of Nestorius and issued an official apology.

# CHAPTER 12

# Socinus

## The Trinity Is Irrelevant and Jesus's Death Is Only an Example

### You Should Know

- The elevation of human reason over church tradition and Scripture was the preeminent presupposition of the Socinian theological system.

- Socinus called upon believers to reject "every interpretation which is repugnant to *right reason*."

- The four purposes of human teachers according to the Racovian Catechism: to help the illiterate or unlearned masses to understand Scripture; to collect the various Scriptures into a logical argument; to encourage people to act on what they know; to aid in dealing with the more difficult passages of Scripture

- The virtue or energy flowing from God was the Holy Spirit, according to Socinus.

- Two major conclusions the Catholic Church reached about Socinianism: it confirmed the church's fears about making the Scriptures available to the laity; it demonstrated the intellectual and theological extremes that could be reached without the stabilizing effects of the authority of tradition

### Essay Questions

*Short*

1. How did Socinus view God's nature? How did he understand the identities of the Father, Son, and Holy Spirit?

2. What, in Socinus's view, did the death of Christ accomplish? How does this differ from the orthodox view?

3. How did the Roman Catholic Church respond to Socinianism? How did Protestants respond to Socinianism?

### Long

1. Summarize Socinus's theological errors. How do these contrast with the teachings of Scripture? What effects are still felt from his influence today?

## Quiz

1. (T/F) According to Socinus, only the Son is truly and fully divine.

2. Socinus claimed that Jesus received the unique, divinely appointed office of _____, though he was not divine.
   - a) Emperor
   - b) Logos
   - c) Priest
   - d) Prophet

3. Socinus's last and most influential work was the _____.
   - a) Racovian Catechism
   - b) Chalcedonian definition
   - c) Socinian Proclamation
   - d) *Institutes*

4. (T/F) Socinians rejected anything that could not be explained or understood by human reason.

5. (T/F) Socinus defended terms like "Trinity" and "original sin" even though they didn't appear in Scripture.

6. (T/F) Socinus held that Jesus was a man who was adopted by God for a special work.

7. (T/F) On Socinus's view, Jesus's death was an atoning sacrifice for the sins of the world.

8. (T/F) For the most part, the Protestant Reformers were sympathetic with Socinus's teachings.

9. King James ordered all copies of the _____ burned with the hope of weeding out anti-Trinitarian theologies.

    a) Bible
    b) Racovian Catechism
    c) *Institutes*
    d) Ninety-five Theses

10. By far the strongest legacy of Socinianism can be found in _____ in the interpretation of Scripture.

    a) The encouragement to persevere
    b) A hesitation to be too confident
    c) The elevation of human reason
    d) The eagerness to apply science

# Conclusion

## Essay Questions

### Short

1. Do you think there is too much or too little emphasis on doctrine today? What should we do to change this situation for the better?

2. How can we avoid being too quick to call an unusual belief "heresy"? Is there something that you used to believe was heresy but that you have changed your mind about?

3. Do you recite creeds in your church? Can these help people avoid false theological beliefs?

4. Do you agree with Justin Holcomb that the Nicene Creed is the best test for orthodoxy?

### Long

1. How would you respond to someone who asked, "Why does it even matter if we believe the right things about God as long as we love God and other people?" Give two or three reasons.

# Notes